Watching the Weather

Clouds

Elizabeth Miles

www.heinemann.co.uk/library

To order:
☎ Phone 44 (0) 1865 888066
📄 Send a fax to 44 (0) 1865 314091
💻 Visit the Heinemann Bookshop at www.heinemann.co.uk/library to browse our catalogue and order online.

First published in Great Britain by Heinemann Library, Halley Court, Jordan Hill, Oxford OX2 8EJ, part of Harcourt Education.
Heinemann is a registered trademark of Harcourt Education Ltd.

Editorial: Nicole Irving and Tanvi Rai
Design: Richard Parker and Celia Jones
Illustrations: Jeff Edwards
Picture Research: Rebecca Sodergren and Mica Brancic
Production: Séverine Ribierre

Originated by Dot Gradations Ltd.
Printed and bound in China by South China Printing Company

ISBN 0 431 19022 4
09 08 07 06 05
10 9 8 7 6 5 4 3 2 1

British Library Cataloguing in Publication Data
Miles, Elizabeth
 Clouds. – (Watching the weather)
 551.5'76
A full catalogue record for this book is available from the British Library.

Acknowledgements
The Publishers would like to thank the following for permission to reproduce photographs: Alamy Images p. **27**; Corbis pp. **i**, **17**; Corbis/Charles & Josette Lenars p. **4**; Corbis/Charles O'Rear p. **7**; Corbis/Galen Rowell p. **11**; Corbis/George Hall p. **25**; Corbis/Jim Reed p. **13**; Corbis/Lester Lefkowitz p. **26**; Corbis/Pat Doyle p. **20**; Corbis/RF p. **5**, **18**, **22**; Corbis/Richard Hutchings p. **16b**; Getty Images/PhotoDisc pp. **23**, **16t**; Getty/Taxi pp. **6**, **9**; Harcourt Education Ltd/Tudor photography p. **29**; Philip Perry/Corbis/Frank Lane Picture Agency p. **24**; Philip Parkhouse p. **28**; Robert Harding Picture Library Ltd pp.**15**, **19**, **21**; Science Photo Library/Pekka Parviainen p. **10**; SPL/Peter Menzel p. **12**.

Cover photograph of clouds reproduced with permission of Corbis.

The Publishers would like to thank Daniel Ogden for his assistance in the preparation of this book.

Every effort has been made to contact copyright holders of any material reproduced in this book. Any omissions will be rectified in subsequent printings if notice is given to the Publishers.

The paper used to print this book comes from sustainable resources.

Contents

Any words appearing in the text in bold, **like this**, are explained in the Glossary.

 Find out more about clouds at www.heinemannexplore.co.uk

What are clouds?

Clouds are made of billions of tiny drops of water called **droplets**. They can be white and fluffy or thick and grey. Clouds sometimes fill the sky.

Clouds form in skies all around the Earth.
Winds blow the clouds about. Clouds
bring us all kinds of weather, such as
rain and snow.

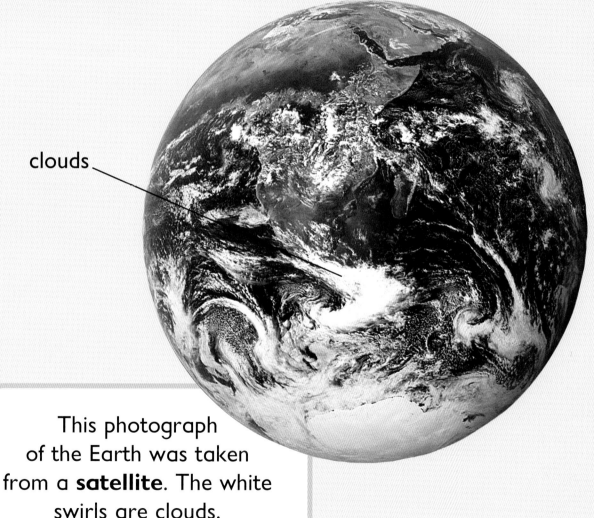

clouds

This photograph
of the Earth was taken
from a **satellite**. The white
swirls are clouds.

Different kinds of clouds

The names of clouds depend on their shape and how high they are in the sky. High, wispy clouds are called cirrus.

Cirrus clouds like these are sometimes called mares' tails because they are shaped like horses' tails. (A mare is a female horse.)

Different kinds of clouds go with different weather. You often see wispy cirrus clouds and low, puffy cumulus clouds in fine, sunny weather. Tall cumulonimbus clouds bring thunderstorms.

Flat, grey clouds like this are called stratus. They may bring rain.

Where do clouds come from?

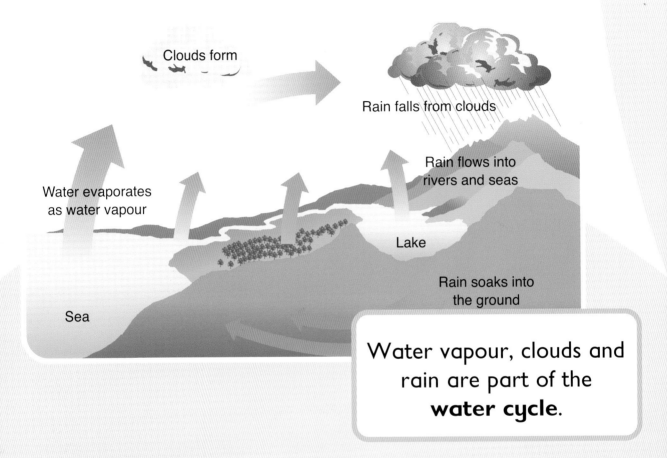

Clouds form

Rain falls from clouds

Rain flows into rivers and seas

Water evaporates as water vapour

Lake

Rain soaks into the ground

Sea

Water vapour, clouds and rain are part of the **water cycle**.

Clouds come from **water vapour** in the air. As water vapour rises in the sky, it gets colder. Then it **condenses** (changes into water **droplets**). These droplets form the clouds.

You often see clouds above mountains. This is because the air gets colder as it moves up the side of the mountain. Water vapour condenses and forms the clouds.

This mountain in South Africa is called Table Mountain. People say the clouds on top look like a tablecloth!

Studying the clouds

When you see these fluffy, white cirrocumulus clouds it is called a mackerel sky. They look like the blotchy markings on a mackerel fish.

Weather forecasters can study clouds to work out what the weather will be like. Cirrocumulus clouds in the sky may mean wet weather is on its way.

Huge, towering clouds like these are called cumulonimbus. Weather forecasters study these clouds because they sometimes bring thunder and lightning.

These clouds can sometimes bring stormy weather.

Measuring the clouds

Weather forecasters use many different ways to understand the weather. To do this they sometimes have to fly inside clouds to study them.

Special aircraft fly straight through storm clouds to collect measurements about the weather.

Weather balloons measure things like **temperature** and **humidity** in clouds. Weather forecasters use the information to write weather forecasts for radio and television.

In this picture, weather scientists are launching a weather balloon into a thunderstorm.

Rain clouds

Air is always swirling around in a cloud. The air gets colder as it rises and warmer as it falls.

Ice crystals form

Falling air warms up

Rising air cools

Water droplets

Rain clouds hold lots of tiny water **droplets**. At the top of the cloud it is very cold. The water droplets here may **freeze** into **ice crystals**.

Water droplets in a cloud join together and get bigger. When they are too big and heavy to stay in the cloud, they fall to the ground as rain.

Snow and hail

Ice crystals like these stick together to make snowflakes.

Snow falls out of clouds when the air is very cold. Tiny **ice crystals** form at the top of the cloud. As they fall, the cold air stops them from melting into **droplets** of rain and we get snow.

Sometimes, the water in clouds **freezes** and we get balls of hard ice called hail. When hail falls on the roof and windows it can make quite a loud noise.

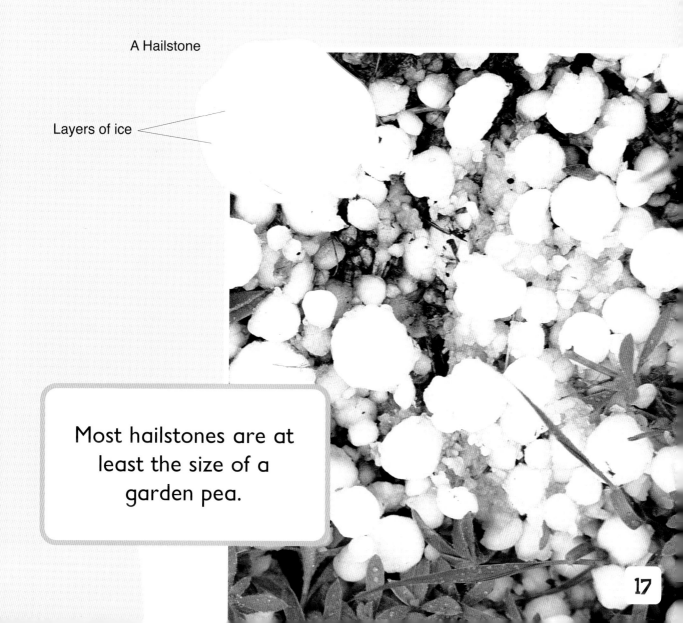

A Hailstone

Layers of ice

Most hailstones are at least the size of a garden pea.

Thunderstorm clouds

Thunderstorm clouds are big, dark clouds that bring storms. Claps of thunder and flashes of lightning fill the sky. The flashes of lightning happen because of a build-up of **electricity** in the cloud.

The powerful heat from a flash of lightning causes a clap of thunder.

You should stay indoors during a thunderstorm.

During a thunderstorm, the sky becomes dark with thunderstorm clouds. Along with thunder and lightning, you often get strong winds and heavy rain.

Cloudy views

This photograph was taken from an aircraft window. A thick covering of cloud hides the ground below.

You cannot see through a thick layer of clouds. When aircraft fly through thick clouds, the pilots sometimes use **radar** to find their way.

Fog is low cloud that rests on the ground. It often forms during the night. In the morning, driving to work through the fog can be dangerous.

It is hard for drivers to see other cars in fog. They must drive slowly to be safe.

Disaster: tornadoes and hurricanes

Tornadoes develop when the centre of a giant storm cloud starts to spin. A twisting column of air stretches down from the cloud to the ground.

A tornado can destroy anything in its path.

During a hurricane, huge waves can sweep across shores and destroy boats and buildings.

Hurricanes bring storm clouds, heavy rain and strong winds. They form over oceans and stretch for hundreds of kilometres. The strong winds can make huge waves at sea.

Unusual clouds

Clouds can be very beautiful. Sometimes the water **droplets** in clouds break up the sunshine into lots of different colours.

These cirrocumulus clouds show shades of pink and blue in them.

People say that these kinds of clouds look like a pile of plates!

Clouds take on unusual shapes. They can look very lumpy or smooth, very flat or piled up. Mountain winds sometimes make piles of clouds called altocumulus lenticularis.

Is it a cloud?

A low layer of dirty cloud over a city may look like cloud, but is it? It might be smog. Smog is a mix of smoke and fog. The smoke comes from the city's factories, cars and homes.

This shows smog over the city of Los Angeles, USA.

An aircraft's narrow trail of ice crystals is called a vapour trail.

Planes high in the sky sometimes make trails that look like long, thin clouds. The plane's engines give out **water vapour**. This can **freeze** into a trail of **ice crystals**.

Project: making clouds

Ask a grown-up to help you. Never touch very hot water or it will burn you.

Clouds are made from **water vapour**. Try making your own water vapour at home.

1. Make sure your bathroom is cold.

2. Close the door and any windows, and block the sink using a rubber plug.

3. Turn on the hot water tap and let the sink fill with hot water.

4. When steam starts to fill the room, look at any cold surfaces, such as a mirror. Can you see any water **droplets** forming?

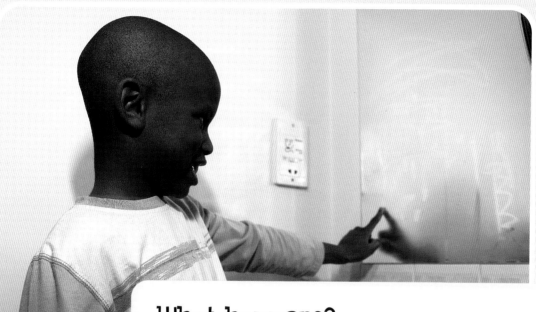

What happens?

Water vapour rises from the hot water. In the cold air, it **condenses** into water droplets to form steam. Bigger water droplets form on cold surfaces such as mirrors. It is droplets like these that form clouds.

Find out more about clouds at
www.heinemannexplore.co.uk

Glossary

condenses changes from a gas (water vapour) to a liquid (water droplets)

droplets very small drops of water

electricity form of energy. Many lights and machines need electricity to make them work.

freeze turn into a very cold solid. For example water freezes into ice.

humidity measure of how much water there is in the air

ice crystals tiny bits of frozen water

radar equipment that uses radio beams to see objects ahead

satellite spacecraft that flies around the Earth carrying equipment like cameras

temperature measure of how hot or cold things are

water cycle way all water keeps moving around as water on land, and in the air

water vapour water in the air. Water vapour is a gas.

weather forecasters people who work out what the weather is going to be like

Find out more

More books to read

Wild Weather: Thunderstorm, Catherine Chambers (Heinemann Library, 2003)

My World of Science: Water, Angela Royston (Heinemann Library, 2001)

What is Weather? Rain, Miranda Ashwell and Andy Owen (Heinemann Library, 1999)

What is Weather? Watching the Weather, Miranda Ashwell and Andy Owen (Heinemann Library, 1999)

Websites to visit

http://www.weatherwizkids.com
A website packed with information about weather features, satellite images from space, games and fun activities to do with the weather.

http://www.planetpals.com/weather.html
Learn more about different sorts of weather and interesting weather facts to share with friends.

Index

Titles in the *Watching the Weather* series include:

Hardback   0 431 19022 4

Hardback   0 431 19023 2

Hardback   0 431 19024 0

Hardback   0 431 19025 9

Hardback   0 431 19026 7

Find out about the other titles in this series on our website www.heinemann.co.uk/library